The Wiersbe
BIBLE STUDY SERIES

The **Wiersbe**
BIBLE STUDY SERIES

Gaining

the Things

That Money

Can't Buy

EPHESIANS

transforming lives together

THE WIERSBE BIBLE STUDY SERIES: EPHESIANS
Published by David C Cook
4050 Lee Vance View
Colorado Springs, CO 80918 U.S.A.

David C Cook Distribution Canada
55 Woodslee Avenue, Paris, Ontario, Canada N3L 3E5

David C Cook U.K., Kingsway Communications
Eastbourne, East Sussex BN23 6NT, England

The graphic circle C logo is a registered trademark of David C Cook.

All Scripture quotations in this study are taken from the *Holy Bible, New
International Version*®. *NIV*®. Copyright © 1973, 1978, 1984 by International
Bible Society. Used by permission of Zondervan. All rights reserved.

In the *Be Rich* excerpts, all Scripture quotations, are taken from
the King James Version of the Bible. (Public Domain.)

All excerpts taken from *Be Rich,* second edition, published by
David C Cook in 2009 © 1979 Warren W. Wiersbe, ISBN 978-1-4347-6734-9

ISBN 978-0-7814-4568-9
eISBN 978-1-4347-0220-3

The Team: Steve Parolini, Karen Lee-Thorp,
Amy Kiechlin, Jack Campbell, and Susan Vannaman
Series Cover Design: John Hamilton Design
Cover Photo: iStockphoto

Printed in the United States of America
First Edition 2009

7 8 9 10 11

081215

Contents

Introduction to Ephesians 7

How to Use This Study 9

Lesson 1
All These Riches (Ephesians 1:1–14) 13

Lesson 2
The Believer's Difference (Ephesians 1:15—2:10) 27

Lesson 3
Peace (Ephesians 2:11–22) 41

Lesson 4
A Mystery Worth Knowing (Ephesians 3:1–13) 55

Lesson 5
What God Has for Us (Ephesians 3:14–21) 69

Lesson 6
Walking in Unity (Ephesians 4) 81

Lesson 7
Imitation (Ephesians 5) 95

Lesson 8
Living It (Ephesians 6) 107

Bonus Lesson
Summary and Review 119

Introduction to Ephesians

The Author

Some names in history we identify immediately, and Paul is one of them. Originally named Saul (Acts 7:58), Paul faithfully served God as a devoted rabbi. As a strong-minded Jew, he became the leader of the anti-Christian movement in Jerusalem, but in the middle of this activity, Saul was "arrested" by Jesus Christ and was converted. He then became Paul, the apostle to the Gentiles.

Around the year AD 53, Paul first ministered in Ephesus, but he did not stay there. Two years later he visited again and remained for two years. During these years he founded a strong church. Nearly ten years later Paul wrote this letter to his beloved friends in Ephesus.

The Saints in Ephesus

Are you surprised that Paul addresses his letter to saints? No word in the New Testament has suffered more than this word *saint*. Even the dictionary defines a saint as a "person officially recognized for holiness of life." Nine times in this brief letter, Paul refers to his readers as saints. The word *saint* is simply one of the many terms used in the New Testament to describe "one who has trusted Jesus Christ as Savior." The person is "alive" physically as well as spiritually.

How did these people become saints? The answer is found in two words: *faithful* and *grace*. Faith and grace go together, because the only way to experience grace is through faith.

The Purpose

Each book in the Bible has its own special theme and message, even though it may deal with many different topics. The theme for the book of Ephesians is the Christian's riches in Christ. Paul examines the source of our blessings, the scope of our blessings, and the sphere of our blessings in this letter.

The fact that Paul is writing about wealth would be significant to his readers, because Ephesus was considered the bank of Asia. The great Temple of Diana, one of the Seven Wonders of the Ancient World, was in Ephesus, and was not only a center for idolatrous worship, but also a depository for wealth. In this letter, Paul compares the church of Jesus Christ to a temple and explains the great wealth that Christ has in His church. Paul is saying to us, "Be Rich!"

—*Warren W. Wiersbe*

How to Use This Study

This study is designed for both individual and small-group use. We've divided it into eight lessons—each references one or more chapters in Warren W. Wiersbe's commentary *Be Rich* (second edition, David C. Cook, 2009). While reading *Be Rich* is not a prerequisite for going through this study, the additional insights and background Wiersbe offers can greatly enhance your study experience.

The **Getting Started** questions at the beginning of each lesson offer you an opportunity to record your first thoughts and reactions to the study text. This is an important step in the study process, because those "first impressions" often include clues about what your heart is longing to discover.

The bulk of the study is found in the **Going Deeper** questions. These dive into the Bible text and, along with excerpts from Wiersbe's commentary, help you examine not only the original context and meaning of the verses but also modern application.

Looking Inward narrows the focus down to your personal story. These intimate questions can be a bit uncomfortable at times, but don't shy away from honesty here. This is where you are asked to stand before the mirror of God's Word and look closely at what you see. It's the place to take a good look at yourself in light of the lesson and search for ways in which you can grow in faith.

Going Forward is the place where you can commit to paper those things you want or need to do in order to better live out the discoveries you made in the Looking Inward section. Don't skip or skim through this. Take the time to really consider what practical steps you might take to move closer to Christ. Then share your thoughts with a trusted friend who can act as an encourager and accountability partner.

Finally, there is a brief **Seeking Help** section to close the lesson. This is a reminder for you to invite God into your spiritual-growth process. If you choose to write out a prayer in this section, come back to it as you work through the lesson and continue to seek the Holy Spirit's guidance as you discover God's will for your life.

Tips for Small Groups

A small group is a dynamic thing. One week it might seem like a group of close-knit friends. The next it might seem more like a group of uncomfortable strangers. A small-group leader's role is to read these subtle changes and adjust the tone of the discussion accordingly.

Small groups need to be safe places for people to talk openly. It is through shared wrestling with difficult life issues that some of the greatest personal growth is discovered. But in order for the group to feel safe, participants need to know it's okay *not* to share sometimes. Always invite honest disclosure, but never force someone to speak if he or she isn't comfortable doing so. (A savvy leader will follow up later with a group member who isn't comfortable sharing in a group setting to see if a one-to-one discussion is more appropriate.)

Have volunteers take turns reading excerpts from Scripture or from the commentary. The more each person is involved even in the mundane tasks, the more they'll feel comfortable opening up in more meaningful ways.

The leader should watch the clock and keep the discussion moving. Sometimes there may be more Going Deeper questions than your group can cover in your available time. If you've had a fruitful discussion, it's okay to move on without finishing everything. And if you think the group is getting bogged down on a question or taken off on a tangent, you can simply say, "Let's go on to question 5." Be sure to save at least ten or fifteen minutes for the Going Forward questions.

Finally, soak your group meetings in prayer—before you begin, during as needed, and always at the end of your time together.

All These Riches
(EPHESIANS 1:1–14)

Before you begin …
- *Pray for the Holy Spirit to reveal truth and wisdom as you go through this lesson.*
- *Read Ephesians 1:1–14. This lesson references chapters 1 and 2 in* Be Rich. *It will be helpful for you to have your Bible and a copy of the commentary available as you work through this lesson.*

Getting Started
From the Commentary

When Jesus Christ wrote His last will and testament for His church, He made it possible for us to share His spiritual riches. Instead of spending it all, Jesus Christ paid it all. His death on the cross and His resurrection make possible our salvation.

He wrote us into His will, then He died so the will would be in force. Then He arose again that He might become the heavenly Advocate (lawyer) to make sure the terms of the will were correctly followed!

—*Be Rich*, page 29

1. What does it mean to be "adopted" by God the Father? What are the spiritual riches we are offered because of that adoption?

More to Consider: Take a moment to think about adoption as we understand the concept in today's world. How is the world's view of adoption similar to or different from what Paul means when he describes God's adoption of His children?

2. Choose one verse or phrase from Ephesians 1:1–14 that stands out to you. This could be something you're intrigued by, something that makes you uncomfortable, something that puzzles you, something that resonates with you, or just something you want to examine further. Write that here. What strikes you about this verse?

Going Deeper

From the Commentary

He has chosen us (v. 4). This is the marvelous doctrine of *election*, a doctrine that has confused some and confounded others. A seminary professor once said to me, "Try to explain election and you may lose your mind. But try to explain it away and you may lose your soul!" That salvation begins with God, and not with man, all Christians will agree. "Ye have not chosen me, but I have chosen you" (John 15:16). The lost sinner, left to his own ways, does not seek God (Rom. 3:10–11); God in His love seeks the sinner (Luke 19:10).

—*Be Rich*, pages 29–30

3. What does Paul mean in Ephesians 1:4 when he says God "chose us" before the creation of the world? What makes the concept of "election" difficult to understand? Why is it critical to seek to understand this tenet of faith?

From the Commentary

> Note that God chose us even before He created the universe, so that our salvation is wholly of His grace and not on the basis of anything we ourselves have done. He chose us *in Christ*, not in ourselves. And He chose us for a purpose: to be holy and without blame. In the Bible, election is always *unto* something. It is a privilege that carries a great responsibility.
>
> Does the sinner respond to God's grace against his own will? No, he responds because God's grace makes him willing to respond. The mystery of divine sovereignty and human responsibility will never be solved in this life. Both are taught in the Bible (John 6:37). Both are true, and both are essential.
>
> —*Be Rich*, page 30

4. Read Ephesians 1:11–14. How do the two apparent contradictions of being chosen and choosing to believe create a mystery worth knowing? Why doesn't God's sovereignty negate man's responsibility? Why are both essential?

From the History Books

The concept of predestination is often associated with Protestant reformer John Calvin, but the theological concept of God's sovereignty was originally examined by Augustine of Hippo in the fifth century AD. While the early church almost universally held up the idea of "free will," Augustine posed the idea that God's grace is granted based on His foreknowledge of the human desire to gain salvation.

5. What are the most significant implications of predestination? What is appealing about the concept of predestination? What are the challenges to understanding this idea? How might free will and predestination work together?

From the Commentary

Adoption has a dual meaning, both present and future. You do not get into God's family by adoption. You get into His family by regeneration, the new birth (John 3:1–18; 1 Peter 1:22–25). Adoption is the act of God by which He gives His "born ones" an adult standing in the family. Why does He do this? So that we might *immediately* begin to claim our inheritance and enjoy our spiritual wealth! A baby cannot legally use this inheritance (Gal. 4:1–7), but an adult son can—and should! This means that you do not have to wait until you are an old saint before you can claim your riches in Christ.

The *future* aspect of adoption is found in Romans 8:22–23, the glorified body we will have when Jesus returns.

—*Be Rich*, page 31

6. Describe the "now" and "not yet" aspects of adoption. What are some of the present riches that Christians gain immediately after they've been "adopted"? How does (or should) this affect the way Christians live today?

From the Commentary

This letter has much to say about God's plan for His people, a plan that was not fully understood even in Paul's day. The word *mystery* has nothing to do with things eerie. It means a "sacred secret, once hidden but now revealed to God's people." We believers are a part of God's "inner circle." We are able to share in the secret that God will one day unite everything in Christ. Ever since sin came into the world, things have been falling apart. First, man was separated from God (Gen. 3). Then man was separated from man, as Cain killed Abel (Gen. 4). People tried to maintain a kind of unity by building the Tower of Babel (Gen. 11), but God judged them and scattered them across the world. God called Abraham and put a difference between the Jew and the Gentile, a difference that was maintained until Christ's death on the cross. Sin is tearing everything apart, but in Christ, God will gather everything together in the culmination of the ages. We are a part of this great eternal program.

—*Be Rich*, pages 32–33

7. What is the "sacred secret"? What are some of the things Paul reveals in Ephesians about God's plan for His people? How does being part of God's "inner circle" affect the way we should reach out to those who don't yet know Christ? How do we keep the "inner circle" idea from becoming a barrier?

From the Commentary

He has sealed us (v. 13). The entire process of salvation is given in this verse, so we had better examine it carefully. It tells how the sinner becomes a saint. First, he hears the gospel of salvation. This is the good news that Christ died for our sins, was buried, and rose again (1 Cor. 15:1ff.). The Ephesians were Gentiles, and the gospel came "to the Jew first" (Rom. 1:16). But Paul, a Jew, brought the gospel to the Gentiles as he shared the Word of God with them.

The Ephesians "heard the gospel" and discovered it was for them—"your salvation" (Eph. 1:13). Even though the Bible teaches election, it also announces, "Go ye into all the world, and preach the gospel to every creature" (Mark 16:15). A soul winner does not discuss election with unsaved people, because it is a family secret that belongs to the saints.

—*Be Rich*, pages 33–34

8. Why are Christians called to preach the gospel if the idea of election is true? How is this an example of obedience? Of God's sovereignty? Of His mystery?

More to Consider: Verse 14 says that God has given us an "earnest" (KJV). In Paul's day, it meant "the down payment to guarantee the final purchase of some commodity or a piece of property." Even today you will hear a real-estate agent talk about earnest money. In what ways is the gift of the Holy Spirit like "earnest money"?

From the Commentary

Did you notice that after each of the main sections in Ephesians 1:4–14, Paul added the purpose behind these gifts? Why has God the Father chosen us, adopted us, and accepted us? "To the praise of the glory of his grace" (Eph. 1:6). Why has the Son redeemed us, forgiven us, revealed God's will to us, and made us part of God's inheritance? "That we should be to the praise of his glory" (Eph. 1:12). Why has God the Spirit sealed us and become the guarantee of our future blessing? "Unto the praise of his glory" (Eph. 1:14).

We often have the idea that God saves sinners mainly because He pities them or wants to rescue them from eternal judgment, but God's main purpose is that He might be glorified.

—*Be Rich*, page 36

9. What does it mean that God's main purpose is to glorify Himself? According to Ephesians, what role do Christians play in that? Why do you think Paul focuses so much in this passage on God's glory?

From the Commentary

> There is always more spiritual wealth to claim from the
> Lord as we walk with Him. The Bible is our guidebook;
> the Holy Spirit is our Teacher. As we search the Word of
> God, we discover more and more of the riches we have
> in Christ. These riches were planned by the Father, pur-
> chased by the Son, and presented by the Spirit. There is
> really no need for us to live in poverty when all of God's
> wealth is at our disposal!
>
> —*Be Rich*, page 37

10. What are some of the riches that Christians can discover in Christ? How
does this truth about riches in Christ speak to those people who are poor in
material things? Those who are wealthy?

Looking Inward

Take a moment to reflect on all that you've explored thus far in this study
of Ephesians 1:1–14. Review your notes and answers and think about how
each of these things matters in your life today.

Tips for Small Groups: To get the most out of this section, form pairs or trios and have group members take turns answering these questions. Be honest and as open as you can in this discussion, but most of all, be encouraging and supportive of others. Be sensitive to those who are going through particularly difficult times and don't press for people to speak if they're uncomfortable doing so.

11. How does being adopted into God's family affect you personally? For example, what are the practical results of this adoption? What is the emotional impact? How does adoption by Christ affect your daily routine? The way you interact with family? Friends? Believers? Nonbelievers?

12. What is the most difficult thing for you to understand about the relationship between "election" and "man's responsibility"? How would you respond to someone who says, "Nothing we do matters, because God already preordained everything"?

13. What are some of the riches you have already experienced because of being adopted into Christ's kingdom? What are some new discoveries about God that have come since your adoption? What are some of the hopes you have for this "kingdom life" that you have been granted?

Going Forward

14. Think of one or two things that you have learned that you'd like to incorporate into your life in the coming week. Remember that this is all about quality, not quantity. It's better to focus on one specific area of life and do it well than to work on many and do poorly (or to be so overwhelmed that you simply don't try).

Do you need to focus on what it means to be adopted by Christ? Do you need to better learn what it means to be responsible for your own actions? Do you need to offer thanks to God for selecting you? Be specific.

Go back through Ephesians 1:1–14 and put a star next to the phrase or verse that speaks to the area you most need to work on. Consider memorizing this verse.

Real-Life Application Ideas: Research the theological concept of predestination (Calvinism is the most well-known form) and meet with fellow believers to discuss it. Follow up that discussion with a talk about the various opportunities you have in your everyday life to share the good news with others. Come up with practical ways you can be obedient to God in sharing that good news.

Seeking Help

15. Write a prayer below (or simply pray one in silence), inviting God to work on your mind and heart in those areas you've previously noted. Be honest about your desires and fears.

Notes for Small Groups:

- *Look for ways to put into practice the things you wrote in the Going Forward section. Talk with other group members about your ideas and commit to being accountable to one another.*
- *During the coming week, ask the Holy Spirit to continue to reveal truth to you from what you've read and studied.*
- *Before you start the next lesson, read Ephesians 1:15— 2:10. For more in-depth lesson preparation, read chapters 3 and 4, "Read the Bank Book" and "Get Out of the Graveyard," in* Be Rich.

The Believer's Difference

(EPHESIANS 1:15—2:10)

Before you begin ...
- *Pray for the Holy Spirit to reveal truth and wisdom as you go through this lesson.*
- *Read Ephesians 1:15—2:10. This lesson references chapters 3 and 4 in* Be Rich. *It will be helpful for you to have your Bible and a copy of the commentary available as you work through this lesson.*

Getting Started

From the Commentary

We discovered that we were "born rich" when we trusted Christ. But this is not enough, for we must grow in our understanding of our riches if we are ever going to use them to the glory of God. Too many Christians have never "read the bankbook" to find out the vast spiritual wealth that God has put to their account through Jesus Christ. They are like the late newspaper publisher William Randolph Hearst, who invested a fortune collecting art treasures from around the world. One day Mr. Hearst found a description of some valuable items that he felt he must own, so he sent his agent abroad to find them. After months of searching, the agent reported that he had finally found the treasures. They were in Mr. Hearst's warehouse.

—*Be Rich*, pages 41–42

1. What are we meant to learn from the story about William Randolph Hearst? How do Christians grow in their understanding of the riches made available to them through Christ?

More to Consider: The Christian life has two dimensions: faith toward God and love toward people. How can the gifts God offers through Christ affect each of these dimensions?

2. Choose one verse or phrase from Ephesians 1:15—2:10 that stands out to you. This could be something you're intrigued by, something that makes you uncomfortable, something that puzzles you, something that resonates

with you, or just something you want to examine further. Write that here. What strikes you about this verse?

Going Deeper

From the Commentary

> That they might know God (1:17b). This, of course, is the highest knowledge possible. The *atheist* claims there is no God for us to know, and the *agnostic* states that if there is a God we cannot know Him. But Paul has met God in the person of Jesus Christ, and he knows that a man really cannot understand much of anything else without a knowledge of God.
>
> —*Be Rich*, page 43

3. Out of all the things Paul could pray for the Ephesians, he's praying for them to know God better (1:17). Why do you suppose that's his top prayer priority?

More to Consider: Paul says he has not stopped giving thanks since he heard about the Ephesians' faith (1:15–16). What do you think this meant in practical terms? What does this suggest about how we ought to pray for others?

From the Commentary

Paul wanted us to understand the hope that is ours because of this [holy] calling (Eph. 4:4). Some callings offer no hope, but the calling we have in Christ assures us of a delightful future. Keep in mind that the word *hope* in the Bible does not mean "I hope so," like a child hoping for a doll or a bike at Christmas. The word carries with it "assurance for the future." The believer's hope is, of course, the return of Jesus Christ for His church (1 Thess. 4:13–18; 1 John 3:1–3). When we were lost, we were "without hope" (Eph. 2:12 NIV), but in Jesus Christ, we have a "living hope" (1 Peter 1:3 NIV) that encourages us day by day.

—*Be Rich*, page 44

4. What are some callings that have no hope? What does the word *hope* mean to nonbelievers? How is the hope that Christians have in Christ different from a nonbeliever's hope? What does the phrase "living hope" mean?

From the History Books

History is rife with stories of individuals and even entire nations that had every reason to lose hope because of war, poverty, or oppression. But despite the challenges they faced, some managed to make it through to the other side and find a happy ending. This is the case for many Jews who were saved from Nazi Germany by people such as Corrie ten Boom, a Christian woman who risked her own life to harbor refugees in her home. She and others like her gave hope to people who otherwise felt hopeless.

5. How is the sort of hope offered by Corrie ten Boom like or unlike the hope offered by faith in Christ? How might Corrie's own hope have played a role in the decisions she made to risk everything to help others? How can our hope in Christ touch those who don't know Christ?

From the Commentary

The unbeliever is not sick; he is dead! He does not need resuscitation; he needs resurrection. All lost sinners are dead, and the only difference between one sinner and another is the state of decay. The lost derelict on skid row may be more decayed outwardly than the unsaved society leader, but both are dead in sin—and one corpse cannot be more dead than another! This means that our world is one vast graveyard, filled with people who are dead while they live (1 Tim. 5:6).

—Be Rich, page 52

6. What is your initial reaction to Wiersbe's statement above? How does a "dead person" discover hope? What implications does our "vast graveyard" world have for believers who *do* have hope in Christ?

From the Commentary

Is it any wonder that the unsaved person is disobedient to God? He is controlled by the world, the flesh, and the Devil, the three great enemies of God! And he cannot change his own nature or, of himself, overcome the world and the Devil. He needs outside help, and that help can come only from God.

—Be Rich, page 54

7. According to 2:1–3, why do sinners behave like sinners? Why is it impossible for a person to overcome the world, the flesh, and the Devil on his or her own? How does this relate to what you learned in the last chapter about God's election?

From the Commentary

Love is one of God's intrinsic attributes, but when this love is related to sinners, it becomes *grace* and *mercy*. God is "rich in mercy" (Eph. 2:4) and in "grace" (Eph. 2:7), and these riches make it possible for sinners to be saved. It comes as a shock to some people when they discover that we are not saved "by God's love," but by God's mercy and grace. In His mercy, He does not give us what we do deserve, and in His grace He gives us what we do not deserve. And all of this is made possible because of the death of Jesus Christ on the cross. It was at Calvary that God displayed His hatred for sin and His love for sinners (Rom. 5:8; John 3:16).

—*Be Rich*, page 55

8. What do sinners deserve? Why? What does God's grace give us that we don't deserve? How does this idea go against the grain of our culture?

Where do you see grace and mercy enacted in our culture today? Where are some places they are sorely needed and yet not known?

9. We are saved by God's grace. What role does our faith play in our salvation (2:8)?

More to Consider: Paul makes it clear in Ephesians 2:8, Colossians 2:13–14, and 2 Timothy 3:14–15 that we can't work our way to salvation—that the work has already been done by God (through Jesus Christ) on our behalf. So if this is true, why do so many people still try to work their way to salvation? What is their motivation to do this?

From the Commentary

Too many Christians think that conversion is the only important experience, and that nothing follows. But this is wrong. We can use the resurrection of Lazarus as an example. After Jesus raised Lazarus from the dead, He said, "Loose him, and let him go" (John 11:44). In other words, "This man is now alive. Get him out of the graveclothes!" Paul had this concept in mind in Ephesians 4:22–24 when he wrote, "That ye put off concerning the former conversation [behavior] the old man, which is corrupt … and that ye put on the new man, which after God is created in righteousness and true holiness." Colossians 3:1 has the same message: "[Since] ye then be risen with Christ, seek those things which are above."

The same resurrection power that saved you and took you out of the graveyard of sin can daily help you live for Christ and glorify Him. At great expense to Himself, God worked for us on the cross. And today, on the basis of that price paid at Calvary, He is working in us to conform us to Christ.

—*Be Rich*, pages 57–58

10. In what ways do Christians often "stay in their graveclothes"? How do Christians tap into the resurrection power God offers? What does "conform us to Christ" mean? In what ways is God working in us to conform us to Christ?

From the Commentary

> The "works" Paul wrote about in Ephesians 2:10 have two special characteristics. First, they are "good" works, in contrast to "works of darkness" and "wicked works." If you contrast Ephesians 2:10 with Ephesians 2:2 you will see that the unbeliever has Satan working in him, and therefore his works are not good. But the believer has God working in him, and therefore his works are good. His works are not good because he himself is good, but because he has a new nature from God, and because the Holy Spirit works in him and through him to produce these good works.
>
> *—Be Rich*, page 59

11. How can you tell the difference between "good" works and "works of darkness" or "wicked works"? If God is the Author of good works, is it possible for a nonbeliever to do good works? Why or why not?

Looking Inward

Take a moment to reflect on all that you've explored thus far in this study of Ephesians 1:15—2:10. Review your notes and answers and think about how each of these things matters in your life today.

Tips for Small Groups: To get the most out of this section, form pairs or trios and have group members take turns answering these questions. Be honest and as open as you can in this discussion, but most of all, be encouraging and supportive of others. Be sensitive to those who are going through particularly difficult times and don't press people to speak if they're uncomfortable doing so.

12. Describe your personal experience with unbelief or the unbelief of friends, family members, or coworkers. What do you think are the greatest obstacles to accepting the good news? Even though it is God's work that changes people's hearts, how might God use you to prepare others for that work?

13. When have you felt hopeless? Where do you turn during these times? How does faith in God turn hopelessness into hope? How might your past experience with hopelessness benefit your outreach to nonbelievers?

14. What are some ways (if any) that you're staying in your graveclothes? What keeps you there? What would it take to start living and take advantage of the resurrection power of Christ?

Going Forward

15. Think of one or two things that you have learned that you'd like to act on in the coming week. Remember that this is all about quality, not quantity. It's better to take action in one specific area of life and do it well than to work on many and do poorly (or to be so overwhelmed that you simply don't try).

Do you need to be more available to friends who don't believe in God, to model or offer hope to them? Be specific. Go back through Ephesians 1:15—2:10 and put a star next to the phrase or verse that speaks to the area you most need to work on. Consider memorizing this verse.

Real-Life Application Ideas: Invite a nonbeliever friend to lunch or dinner to talk about faith issues. Make it clear in your invitation that you're not going to try to "convert" this person—that you're really just very interested in what prompts that agnosticism or atheism. Then be sure to follow through by doing what you said—not offering judgment, simply listening and trusting that God might use your conversation for His purposes.

Seeking Help

16. Write a prayer below (or simply pray one in silence), inviting God to work on your mind and heart in those areas you've previously noted. Be honest about your desires and fears.

Notes for Small Groups:

- *Look for ways to put into practice the things you wrote in the Going Forward section. Talk with other group members about your ideas and commit to being accountable to one another.*

- *During the coming week, ask the Holy Spirit to continue to reveal truth to you from what you've read and studied.*

- *Before you start the next lesson, read Ephesians 2:11–22. For more in-depth lesson preparation, read chapter 5, "The Great Peace Mission," in* Be Rich.

Peace
(EPHESIANS 2:11–22)

Before you begin ...
- *Pray for the Holy Spirit to reveal truth and wisdom as you go through this lesson.*
- *Read Ephesians 2:11–22. This lesson references chapter 5 in* Be Rich. *It will be helpful for you to have your Bible and a copy of the commentary available as you work through this lesson.*

Getting Started

From the Commentary

It seems that most peace missions fail. I read somewhere that from 1500 BC to AD 850 there were 7,500 "eternal covenants" agreed on among various nations with the hope of bringing peace, but that no covenant lasted longer than two years. The only "eternal covenant" that has lasted—and that will last—is the one made by the eternal God, sealed by the blood of Jesus Christ. It is Christ's peace mission that Paul explained in this section, and three very important words summarize this great work: separation, reconciliation, and unification.

—*Be Rich*, page 65

1. What is your first thought when you hear the word *peace*? In your experience, how difficult is it to find and maintain peace at home? In the workplace? At church?

More to Consider: For years, the Jews looked down on the Gentiles, claiming, among other things, that the physical mark of their covenant with God, circumcision, was proof of their faith. What are some modern-day examples of this sort of flawed thinking?

2. Choose one verse or phrase from Ephesians 2:11–22 that stands out to you. This could be something you're intrigued by, something that makes you uncomfortable, something that puzzles you, something that resonates with you, or just something you want to examine further. Write that here. What strikes you about this verse?

Going Deeper

From the Commentary

> It is worth noting that the spiritual plight of the Gentiles was caused not by God but by their own willful sin. Paul said the Gentiles knew the true God but deliberately refused to honor Him (Rom. 1:18–23). Religious history is not a record of man starting with many gods (idolatry) and gradually discovering the one true God.
>
> Rather, it is the sad story of man knowing the truth about God and deliberately turning away from it! It is a story of devolution, not evolution! The first eleven chapters of Genesis give the story of the decline of the Gentiles, and from Genesis 12 on (the call of Abraham), it is the story of the Jews. God separated the Jews from the Gentiles that He might be able to save the Gentiles also. "Salvation is of the Jews" (John 4:22).
>
> —*Be Rich*, page 67

3. What is your reaction to Wiersbe's explanation of the Gentiles' story as "devolution"? How did God use the Jews to save the Gentiles?

From the Commentary

The word *reconcile* means "to bring together again." A distraught husband wants to be reconciled to his wife who has left him; a worried mother longs to be reconciled to a wayward daughter; and the lost sinner needs to be reconciled to God. Sin is the great separator in this world. It has been dividing people since the very beginning of human history. When Adam and Eve sinned, they were separated from God. Before long, their sons were separated from each other and Cain killed Abel. The earth was filled with violence (Gen. 6:5–13), and the only remedy seemed to be judgment. But even after the flood, men sinned against God and each other, and even tried to build their own unity without God's help. The result was another judgment that scattered the nations and confused the tongues. It was then that God called Abraham, and through the nation of Israel, Jesus Christ came to the world. It was His work on the cross that abolished the enmity between Jew and Gentile and between sinners and God.

—*Be Rich*, page 68

4. As you consider this progression, what stands out about the role God has played in reconciliation? What stands out about humanity's role? How does Jesus' work on the cross differ from the other ways God reached out to man?

From the History Books

When the police officers who had been videotaped beating Rodney King after a traffic stop were acquitted of any wrongdoing, the public outrage that followed sparked the 1992 Los Angeles riots. Tensions were already high between the black community and the LAPD, but the acquittal quickly escalated that tension. On the third day of the riots, King himself went before the camera to appeal for an end to the violence, asking the rather simple, yet pointed question, "Can't we get along?"

5. What are the root causes of tension between people? How are those root causes present in the story of the Los Angeles riots, or in other stories of wars or disagreements you can think of? Why is it so easy for tensions to erupt into something violent before a peaceful solution is found?

From the Commentary

In Jesus Christ, Jew and Gentile become one. "He is our peace" (Eph. 2:14). Through Christ, the far-off Gentile is made "nigh" (Eph. 2:13, 17), and both Jew and Gentile are made one. The consequences of Christ's work are, then, the destroying of the enmity by the abolishing of the law, and the creating of a new *man*—the church, the body of Christ.

—*Be Rich*, page 70

6. What does "abolishing of the law" mean in this context? What law was abolished, and how? How did abolishing the law destroy the enmity between Jewish Christians and Gentile Christians? Why is this ability to "become one" unavailable apart from Christ?

From the Commentary

A man stopped in my office one day and said he wanted to get help. "My wife and I need a re-cancellation!" he blurted out. I knew he meant "reconciliation." But in one sense, "re-cancellation" was the right word. They had sinned against each other (and the Lord), and there could be no harmony until those sins were canceled. A God of love wants to reconcile the sinner to Himself, but a God of holiness must see to it that sin is judged. God solved the problem by sending His Son to be the sacrifice for our sins, thereby revealing His love and meeting the demands of His righteousness.

—*Be Rich*, pages 71–72

7. How does Jesus' cancellation of our sins bring us peace with God? How does the once-and-for-all cancellation of sins go together with an ongoing need for repentance?

Paul says our reconciliation with God also reconciles us to our fellow Christians. What are some of the ways he describes our oneness in 2:14–22? If reconciliation is made complete in Jesus, why is there continued strife among Christians of different ethnic groups, denominations, and factions?

From the Commentary

> Israel was God's chosen nation, but they rejected their Redeemer and suffered the consequences. The kingdom was taken from them and given to "a nation bringing forth the fruits thereof" (Matt. 21:43). This "new nation" is the

church, "a chosen generation ... a holy nation, a peculiar people" (Ex. 19:6; 1 Peter 2:9).

—*Be Rich*, page 72

8. The church is "peculiar" in the sense of belonging peculiarly (specially) to God. What are the implications of this for you as an individual? What are the implications for us as the worldwide people of God?

More to Consider: After Jesus' death and resurrection, the temple where God dwells was no longer a building, but the community of those who have trusted God. How do you imagine the Jews responded to this claim? Why did so many Jews choose to reject Jesus as Messiah? Why is it hard to let go of longstanding traditions?

From the Commentary

As you look back over this chapter, you cannot help but praise God for what He, in His grace, has done for sinners. Through Christ, He has raised us from the dead and seated us on the throne. He has reconciled us and set us into His temple. Neither spiritual *death* nor spiritual *distance* can defeat the grace of God! But He has not only saved us individually, He has also made us a part of His church collectively. What a tremendous privilege it is to be a part of God's eternal program!

—*Be Rich*, page 74

9. Why is it significant that God not only saved individuals but also made them part of His church? What does this say about the role of the church in God's overall plan?

From the Commentary

Jesus Christ died to make reconciliation possible. You and I must live to make the message of reconciliation personal. God has "given to us the ministry of reconciliation" (2 Cor. 5:18). We are His ambassadors of peace (2 Cor. 5:20).

—*Be Rich*, page 75

10. What does it mean to be a part of this "ministry of reconciliation"? What does it look like in our everyday world to be ambassadors for peace? How can Christians embody this in ways that affect their communities and the whole world?

Looking Inward

Take a moment to reflect on all that you've explored thus far in this study of Ephesians 2:11–22. Review your notes and answers and think about how each of these things matters in your life today.

> *Tips for Small Groups: To get the most out of this section, form pairs or trios and have group members take turns answering these questions. Be honest and as open as you can in this discussion, but most of all, be encouraging and supportive of others. Be sensitive to those who are going through particularly difficult times and don't press people to speak if they're uncomfortable doing so.*

11. What are some areas of your life where you experience conflict? What are the sources of that conflict? What would a peaceful solution to that conflict look like?

12. How is it important to you that Jesus has made reconciliation with God possible? In what ways does that bring you peace?

13. Do you experience the church as a dwelling for God's Spirit and as a holy nation in which you are a fully active citizen (2:19–22)? Describe your experience. None of us can control what other people do, but what is your part in building peace and holiness in the church?

14. What are some ways you have been an ambassador for Christ? In what areas of your life do you find it most difficult to be a peacemaker?

Going Forward

15. Think of one or two things that you have learned that you'd like to work on in the coming week. Remember that this is all about quality, not quantity. It's better to work on one specific area of life and do it well than to work on many and do poorly (or to be so overwhelmed that you simply don't try).

Do you need to focus on becoming more aware of the peace you have with God? Do you need to act as a peacemaker at home? With other believers? With nonbelievers at work or school? Be specific. Go back through Ephesians 2:11–22 and put a star next to the phrase or verse that speaks to the area you most need to work on. Consider memorizing this verse.

Real-Life Application Ideas: The peace that Jesus brings is first an internal peace that defies understanding. But Jesus' message of peace was meant to cause changes in the way we act, too. Think of some specific areas of conflict in your life where you are not acting in a "peacemaking" manner. Ephesians 2 focuses on peace between Christians, but maybe the key relationship you need to look at is with a nonbeliever. Pray for and decide on a course of action that will bring (or at least offer the possibility of) peace to that situation, then follow that plan.

Seeking Help

16. Write a prayer below (or simply pray one in silence), inviting God to work on your mind and heart in those areas you've previously noted. Be honest about your desires and fears.

Notes for Small Groups:
  - *Look for ways to put into practice the things you wrote in the Going Forward section. Talk with other group members about your ideas and commit to being accountable to one another.*
  - *During the coming week, ask the Holy Spirit to continue to reveal truth to you from what you've read and studied.*
  - *Before you start the next lesson, read Ephesians 3:1–13. For more in-depth lesson preparation, read chapter 6, "I Know a Secret," in* Be Rich.

A Mystery Worth Knowing

(EPHESIANS 3:1–13)

Before you begin ...
- *Pray for the Holy Spirit to reveal truth and wisdom as you go through this lesson.*
- *Read Ephesians 3:1–13. This lesson references chapter 6 in* Be Rich. *It will be helpful for you to have your Bible and a copy of the commentary available as you work through this lesson.*

Getting Started

From the Commentary

Twice in this letter, Paul reminded his readers that he was a prisoner (Eph. 3:1; 4:1), and at the close he called himself an "ambassador in bonds" (Eph. 6:20). No doubt the Ephesians were asking, "Why is Paul a prisoner in Rome? Why would God permit such a thing?" In this paragraph, Paul explained his situation and, in doing so, also explained one of the greatest truths in this letter, the "mystery" of the church.

—*Be Rich,* pages 79–80

1. Why do you think Paul talks about his imprisonment so often? In what ways does explaining his situation answer the question of the "mystery"?

More to Consider: Compare Ephesians 3:1 and 3:14. What "reason" or "cause" (KJV) is Paul referring to? Why is that significant to his explanation of the mystery of the church?

2. Choose one verse or phrase from Ephesians 3:1–13 that stands out to you. This could be something you're intrigued by, something that makes you uncomfortable, something that puzzles you, something that resonates with you, or just something you want to examine further. Write that here. What strikes you about this verse?

Going Deeper

From the Commentary

> Paul was a leader in Jewish orthodoxy when Christ saved
> him (Gal. 1:11–24; Phil. 3:1–11), yet in the providence
> of God, he began his early ministry in a local church in
> Antioch that was composed of both Jews and Gentiles
> (Acts 11:19–26). When the council was held at Jerusalem
> to determine the status of believing Gentiles, Paul coura-
> geously defended the grace of God and the unity of the
> church (Acts 15; Gal. 2:1–10).
>
> —*Be Rich*, pages 80–81

3. How did Paul's background in Jewish orthodoxy help him in his role as a
leader in God's church? Why was it important for Paul to start his ministry
in a church that had a mixed audience? How might experience with an eth-
nically mixed congregation help in the training of Christian leaders today?

From the Commentary

> Paul was not only a "prisoner" because of "the mystery,"
> but he was also a "minister." God gave him a "dispensa-
> tion" (stewardship) that he might go to the Gentiles, not
> only with the good news of salvation through Christ, but
> also with the message that Jews and Gentiles are now one
> in Christ. The word *dispensation* comes from two Greek
> words: *oikos*, meaning "house" and *nomos*, meaning "law."
> Our English word *economy* is derived directly from the
> Greek *oikonomia*, "the law of the house," or "a steward-
> ship, a management." God has different ways of managing
> His program from age to age, and these different "steward-
> ships" Bible students sometimes call "dispensations" (Eph.
> 1:9–10). God's principles do not change, but His meth-
> ods of dealing with humankind do change over the course
> of history.
>
> —*Be Rich*, pages 81–82

4. Paul wrote about the "administration of God's grace" or "dispensation of
the grace of God" (KJV) that had been entrusted to him. According to Ephesians 3:2–6, what was this dispensation of grace that had been entrusted to
Paul? Why was it such a radically new idea that Gentiles could share equally
with Jews in the promise of life in Christ Jesus?

From Today's World

Secrecy has always been attractive to societies. Throughout Christian history, splinter groups have sprung up and claimed to have the one true way to truth that other Christians lack. Many of these also promise secret knowledge available only to the elite or those who have ascended in the ranks of the organization. There are also philanthropic organizations with secret memberships, handshakes, passwords, and initiation rites.

5. What are some different reasons groups choose to be mysterious? What does that mystery do for those people? How is that kind of mystery different from the mystery Paul writes about in Ephesians? How is it similar?

From the Commentary

> Finally, new riches are available to the Gentiles: "the unsearchable riches of Christ" (Eph. 3:8). Paul called them "exceeding riches" (Eph. 2:7), but here he described them as "unfathomable." The words can also be translated "untraceable," which means that they are so vast you cannot discover their end....
>
> Are these riches available to every believer? Yes!
>
> —*Be Rich*, pages 83–84

6. What are these unfathomable riches available to every believer?

7. Paul says it's a huge honor for him to proclaim these unfathomable riches to the Gentiles because he's the least of God's people (3:8). Why do you think it's important for him to tell his readers about his undeserved significance?

From the Commentary

> Perhaps at this point, you are asking yourself the question, "Why did God keep His secret about the church hidden for so many centuries?" Certainly the Old Testament clearly states that God will save the Gentiles through Israel, but nowhere are we told that both Jews and Gentiles will form a new creation, the church, the body of

Christ. It was this mystery that the Spirit revealed to Paul and other leaders in the early church, and that was so difficult for the Jews to accept.

—*Be Rich*, page 84

8. Why do you think it was so difficult for the Jews to accept what the Spirit revealed to Paul (and others)?

9. By what authority does Paul speak in Ephesians? How could his original readers, who didn't have his letter already packaged in something called "the Bible," know that what he said about the Gentiles had authority? How can a person today know that what a leader presents as truth is from God and not simply a construct of man?

From the Commentary

> Certainly the angels know about the power of God as
> seen in His creation. But the wisdom of God as seen in
> His new creation, the church, is something new to them.
> Unsaved men, including wise philosophers, look at God's
> plan of salvation and consider it "foolishness" (1 Cor.
> 1:18–31). But the angels watch the outworking of God's
> salvation, and they praise His wisdom. Paul called it *man-*
> *ifold wisdom.*
>
> —*Be Rich,* page 85

10. What is significant in Paul's explanation of God's "manifold wisdom"
(3:10)? Why do Paul's readers need to understand the angels' perspective
on God's creation, the church? What does this say about the value of the
church?

More to Consider: Read 1 Timothy 1:11 and 2 Timothy 4:7. Accord-
ing to these passages, Paul "kept the faith" and handed it down to
others. What does church history tell us about how these truths have

been handed down? Are there things that have been "lost in transla-tion" over the years? How do those things affect the effectiveness of the church?

From the Commentary

> The reason many churches are weak and ineffective is because they do not understand what they have in Christ. And the cause of this is often spiritual leaders who are not good "stewards of the mystery." Because they do not "rightly divide the word of truth" (2 Tim. 2:15), they confuse their people concerning their spiritual position in Christ, and they rob their people of the spiritual wealth in Christ.
>
> —*Be Rich*, page 87

11. In Ephesians 3:12, Paul mentions something rich we have in Christ. How is this an example of spiritual wealth? How can spiritual leaders become good stewards in educating their people about this wealth?

From the Commentary

> People who do not understand God's "mystery" in His
> church are trying to make spiritual progress with the
> wrong map. Or, to change the figure, they are trying to
> build with the wrong blueprints. God's churches on this
> earth—the local assemblies—are not supposed to be either
> Gentile culture cliques or Jewish culture cliques. For a
> German church to refuse fellowship to a Swede is just as
> unscriptural as for a Jewish congregation to refuse a Gen-
> tile. God's church is not to be shackled by culture, class,
> or any other physical distinction.
>
> —*Be Rich*, page 89

12. What are some of the cultural shackles you've seen in a local church?
What does it take to remove those shackles of culture?

Looking Inward

Take a moment to reflect on all that you've explored thus far in this study
of Ephesians 3:1–13. Review your notes and answers and think about how
each of these things matters in your life today.

Tips for Small Groups: To get the most out of this section, form pairs or trios and have group members take turns answering these questions. Be honest and as open as you can in this discussion, but most of all, be encouraging and supportive of others. Be sensitive to those who are going through particularly difficult times and don't press people to speak if they're uncomfortable doing so.

13. Go through Ephesians 3:1–13 and underline some of the things that define the mystery of the church. What aspects of the mystery do you understand? What about the mystery of the church is difficult for you to understand? What does it feel like to know you have been given access to know this mystery?

14. What are some ways you're helping your local church to be a good steward of the mystery of faith? What are some things you're doing that might cause ineffectiveness? How can you be a positive agent of change in your church?

Going Forward

15. Think of one or two things that you have learned that you'd like to work on in the coming week. Remember that this is all about quality, not quantity. It's better to work on one specific area of life and do it well than to work on many and do poorly (or to be so overwhelmed that you simply don't try).

For example, do you need to reflect more deeply on what it means to be the church, a body that crosses ethnic and cultural boundaries? How do you go about reflecting on that and letting it affect your life? Be specific. Go back through Ephesians 3:1–13 and put a star next to the phrase or verse that speaks to the area you most need to work on. Consider memorizing this verse.

Real-Life Application Ideas: This section of Ephesians is all about the mystery of God's new idea—the church. Meet with other church members to discuss the areas in which your church is doing well in keeping with Paul's guidance, and the areas in which your church might be able to improve. Then discuss both of these with your church leadership.

Seeking Help

16. Write a prayer below (or simply pray one in silence), inviting God to work on your mind and heart in those areas you've previously noted. Be honest about your desires and fears.

Notes for Small Groups:
- *Look for ways to put into practice the things you wrote in the Going Forward section. Talk with other group members about your ideas and commit to being accountable to one another.*
- *During the coming week, ask the Holy Spirit to continue to reveal truth to you from what you've read and studied.*
- *Before you start the next lesson, read Ephesians 3:14–21. For more in-depth lesson preparation, read chapter 7, "Get Your Hands on Your Wealth," in* Be Rich.

What God Has for Us

(EPHESIANS 3:14–21)

Before you begin …

- *Pray for the Holy Spirit to reveal truth and wisdom as you go through this lesson.*
- *Read Ephesians 3:14–21. This lesson references chapter 7 in Be Rich. It will be helpful for you to have your Bible and a copy of the commentary available as you work through this lesson.*

Getting Started

From the Commentary

This passage is the second of two prayers recorded in Ephesians, the first one being Ephesians 1:15–23. In the first prayer, the emphasis is on *enlightenment*, but in this prayer, the emphasis is on *enablement*. It is not so much a matter of *knowing* as *being*—laying our hands on what God has for us and by faith making it a vital part of our lives. Paul was saying, "I want you to get your hands on your wealth, realize how vast it is, and start to use it."

—*Be Rich,* page 93

1. What are the riches of Christ? How do Christians go about laying their hands on these riches and using them? What is the difference between "knowing" and "being" as it relates to the riches of Christ?

More to Consider: Read more of Paul's prison prayers in Philippians 1:9–11 and Colossians 1:9–12. What spiritual conditions does Paul address in these prayers?

2. Choose one verse or phrase from Ephesians 3:14–21 that stands out to you. This could be something you're intrigued by, something that makes you uncomfortable, something that puzzles you, something that resonates with you, or just something you want to examine further. Write that here. What strikes you about this verse?

Going Deeper

From the Commentary

You have noticed, no doubt, the emphasis on spiritual posture in Ephesians. As lost sinners, we were buried in the graveyard (Eph. 2:1). But when we trusted Christ, He raised us from the dead and seated us with Christ in the heavenlies (Eph. 2:4–6). Because we are *seated* with Christ, we can *walk* so as to please Him (Eph. 4:1, 17; 5:2, 8, 15) and we can *stand* against the Devil (Eph. 6:10–13). But the posture that links "sitting" with "walking" and "standing" is "bowing the knee." It is through prayer that we lay hold of God's riches that enable us to behave like Christians and battle like Christians. Whether we actually bow our knees is not the important thing; that we bow our hearts and wills to the Lord and ask Him for what we need is the vital matter.

—*Be Rich*, page 94

3. What does it mean to "bow our hearts" to the Lord? How do we do that? Why is this spiritual posture important enough for Paul to write about?

From the Commentary

> All men are not children of God by nature. Instead, they
> are children of disobedience and children of wrath (Eph.
> 2:2–3). As Creator, God is the Father of each person,
> but as Savior, He is only the Father of those who believe.
> There is no such thing in Scripture as the universal father-
> hood of God that saves all men.
>
> —*Be Rich*, page 95

4. Why is it important to distinguish between God's roles as Creator and as
Savior? How does this affect believers' roles in the lives of nonbelievers?

From Today's World

Depending on your church experience, you may practice a variety of prayer
positions. The Bible itself describes a variety of postures for prayer—everything
from lying prostrate on the floor to standing. A common prayer posture today
is the "head bowed, eyes closed" approach often used in church services and
even practiced in public meetings or around the dinner table, whether at home
or at a restaurant. The "bowed knees" prayer is common to some traditions but
a rare event in others.

5. Does posture matter in prayer? Why or why not? What does Paul's decision to kneel suggest about his prayer? Why is the "bow your head, close your eyes" posture so popular? How might this type of posture affect people's prayer lives?

From the Commentary

What does it mean to have the Holy Spirit empower the inner man? It means that our spiritual faculties are controlled by God, and we are exercising them and growing in the Word (Heb. 5:12–14). It is only when we yield to the Spirit and let Him control the inner man that we succeed in living to the glory of God. This means feeding the inner man the Word of God, praying and worshipping, keeping clean, and exercising the senses by loving obedience.

—*Be Rich*, pages 96–97

6. In his prayer, Paul asks God to strengthen the believers through His Spirit (3:16). How do believers yield to the Spirit? What are some practical ways to feed the inner person God's Word?

From the Commentary

> The trials of life test the depth of our experience. If two
> roommates in college have a falling out, they may seek
> new roommates, for after all, living with a roommate is a
> passing experience. But if a husband and wife, who love
> each other, have a disagreement, the trial only deepens
> their love as they seek to solve the problems. The storm
> that blows reveals the strength of the roots.
>
> —*Be Rich*, page 98

7. In Ephesians 3:17, Paul speaks of being rooted in God's love. What are
the specific things that root believers in God's love? How do trials reveal the
"strength of the roots"? How can believers strengthen those roots to with-
stand greater trials in the future?

From the Commentary

> No Christian ever has to worry about having inadequate
> spiritual resources to meet the demands of life. If he prays
> for spiritual strength and spiritual depth, he will be able to

apprehend—get his hands on—all the resources of God's love and grace. "I can do all things through Christ which strengtheneth me" (Phil. 4:13).

—*Be Rich*, page 99

8. Paul writes in verse 18 about having power "together with all the saints." Power to do what? How do we grab hold of that power? What role does the Holy Spirit play in leading us to discover the power of the saints? What are the results of apprehending the resources of God's love and grace? Where do you see these results in your church?

More to Consider: Read Colossians 2:9–10. What does this passage say about being complete in Christ? If we are already complete, what else must we do to enjoy the resources?

From the Commentary

> Paul seemed to want to use every word possible to convey to us the vastness of God's power as found in Jesus Christ.
>
> —*Be Rich*, page 100

9. Go back through Ephesians 1—3 and circle all the words Paul uses to express God's power. Why do you think Paul emphasizes God's power? What might this say about the audience he is writing to? How would your church benefit from more richly partaking of God's power?

From the Commentary

> Why does God share His power with us? So that we can build great churches for our own glory? So that we can boast of our own achievements? No! "To him be glory in the church!" The Spirit of God was given to glorify the Son of God (John 16:14). The church on earth is here to glorify the Son of God.
>
> —*Be Rich*, pages 101–2

10. In what ways has the church done a good job of glorifying the Son of God? What are some ways the church has failed in this regard? How might your local church remedy those failures in your own community?

Looking Inward

Take a moment to reflect on all that you've explored thus far in this study of Ephesians 3:14–21. Review your notes and answers and think about how each of these things matters in your life today.

> *Tips for Small Groups: To get the most out of this section, form pairs or trios and have group members take turns answering these questions. Be honest and as open as you can in this discussion, but most of all, be encouraging and supportive of others. Be sensitive to those who are going through particularly difficult times and don't press people to speak if they're uncomfortable doing so.*

11. What value do you ascribe to the posture of prayer? How does your prayer posture affect your prayer life? What are some ways you can place more focused attention on your prayer life? How might that help your faith mature?

12. What are some ways you are feeding your inner person? List some of them. When you're making decisions in day-to-day life, how do you know that you're yielding to the Spirit? Or, what are signs that you're not doing this?

13. How and where have you discovered the resources of God's love and grace? How do you see these resources evidenced in your life? If you don't see them active in your life, what might be getting in the way?

Going Forward

14. Think of one or two things that you have learned that you'd like to work on in the coming week. Remember that this is all about quality, not quantity. It's better to work on one specific area of life and do it well than to work on many and do poorly (or to be so overwhelmed that you simply don't try).

Do you want to discover more about how to pray? Do you need to receive and then find ways to apply the gifts God offers? Be specific. Go back through Ephesians 3:14–21 and put a star next to the phrase or verse that speaks to the area you most need to work on. Consider memorizing this verse.

Real-Life Application Ideas: Take a quick personal inventory to examine how well you're enabling the gifts God offers. Then spend time in prayer (choose a prayer posture for this that helps you focus your thoughts) asking God to reveal His gifts and give you wisdom in using them.

Seeking Help

15. Write a prayer below (or simply pray one in silence), inviting God to work on your mind and heart in those areas you've previously noted. Be honest about your desires and fears.

Notes for Small Groups:

- *Look for ways to put into practice the things you wrote in the Going Forward section. Talk with other group members about your ideas and commit to being accountable to one another.*

- *During the coming week, ask the Holy Spirit to continue to reveal truth to you from what you've read and studied.*

- *Before you start the next lesson, read Ephesians 4. For more in-depth lesson preparation, read chapters 8 and 9, "Let's Walk Together" and "Take Off the Graveclothes!" in* Be Rich.

Walking in Unity
(EPHESIANS 4)

Before you begin ...
- *Pray for the Holy Spirit to reveal truth and wisdom as you go through this lesson.*
- *Read Ephesians 4. This lesson references chapters 8 and 9 in* Be Rich. *It will be helpful for you to have your Bible and a copy of the commentary available as you work through this lesson.*

Getting Started
From the Commentary

The main idea in these first sixteen verses is the unity of believers in Christ. This is simply the practical application of the doctrine taught in the first half of the letter: God is building a body, a temple. He has reconciled Jews and Gentiles to Himself in Christ. The oneness of believers in Christ is already a spiritual reality. Our responsibility is to guard, protect, and preserve that unity.

—*Be Rich*, page 106

1. What do you think prompted Paul to focus on the unity theme in Ephesians? What makes this such an important aspect of our faith-life?

More to Consider: Compare and contrast the idea of "unity" with that of "uniformity." What is the goal of unity? Uniformity? Why is the distinction important?

2. Choose one verse or phrase from Ephesians 4 that stands out to you. This could be something you're intrigued by, something that makes you uncomfortable, something that puzzles you, something that resonates with you, or just something you want to examine further. Write that here. What strikes you about this verse?

Going Deeper

From the Commentary

> *Meekness* is not weakness. It is power under control.
>
> —*Be Rich*, page 107

3. In Ephesians 4:1–2, Paul begins to describe how we should live in light of our calling. The first quality he highlights is meekness or humility. In Matthew 11:29, Jesus describes Himself as meek or "humble." How was Jesus' life an example of meekness and humility—that is, power under control, used to serve rather than to dominate?

How do humility and patience work together? What roles do these and other character traits in Ephesians 4:1–3 play in building unity?

From the Commentary

> Paul was quite concerned that Christians not break the
> unity of the Spirit by agreeing with false doctrine (Rom.
> 16:17–20), and the apostle John echoed this warning
> (2 John 6–11). The local church cannot believe in peace at
> any price, for God's wisdom is "first pure, then peaceable"
> (James 3:17). Purity of doctrine of itself does not produce
> spiritual unity, for there are churches that are sound in
> faith, but unsound when it comes to love. This is why Paul
> joined the two: "speaking the truth in love" (Eph. 4:15).
>
> *—Be Rich*, page 110

4. How can false doctrine break the unity of a church? How can we know if
a doctrine is false? Why does purity of doctrine alone not produce unity?

From the History Books

Questionable (or just plain wrong) doctrine has been a staple of Christianity from the very earliest days of the church. But when false doctrine
is combined with so-called love, trouble begins. Cults spring up out of
Christianity and have success in part because they preach a message of love

to people who are hungry for it. However, in reaching for this sense of belonging, unwitting participants ignore or look past doctrine that otherwise would be a big red flag to anyone who knows even just the basics about the Christian faith.

5. What surprises you most about the draw of cults? What is the difference between a church that is cultish and one that simply has a different doctrinal bent than others? How can the church be unified when there are so many doctrinal differences between denominations?

From the Commentary

How does the believer discover and develop his gifts? By fellowshipping with other Christians in the local assembly. Gifts are not toys to play with. They are tools to build with. And if they are not used in love, they become weapons to fight with, which is what happened in the Corinthian church (1 Cor. 12—14). Christians are not to live in isolation, for after all, they are members of the same body.

—*Be Rich*, page 111

6. Respond to the statement: "Gifts are not toys to play with." How do all the gifts in Ephesians 4:11–12 work together to create unity? In what ways do people use their gifts wrongly to create division?

More to Consider: Compare the gifts listed in Ephesians 4:11–12 with those described in 1 Corinthians 12:4–11. Who are some people you know with the various gifts? How do you see them in evidence at your church or in your study group?

From the Commentary

There are some negatives in the Christian life, and here is one of them: "Walk not as other Gentiles walk." The Christian is not to imitate the life of the unsaved people around him. They are "dead in trespasses and sins" (Eph. 2:1), while he has been raised from the dead and been given eternal life in Christ.

—*Be Rich*, pages 119–20

7. What does Paul mean by walking as other Gentiles walk (4:17)? Give some examples. What specific warnings might Paul offer today to Christians who imitate the life of the unsaved? If Christians aren't to walk like other Gentiles, how then should they walk?

From the Commentary

> This was Paul's argument—you no longer belong to the old corruption of sin; you belong to the new creation in Christ. Take off the graveclothes! How do we do this? "Be renewed in the spirit of your mind" (Eph. 4:23). Conversion is a crisis that leads to a process.
>
> —*Be Rich*, page 122

8. How do believers renew the spirit of their minds? What is the process that conversion leads to? Why is this message about the post-conversion process important for new believers?

More to Consider: Read Ephesians 4:25. How can lying lead to disunity in a church? What are some examples of disunity caused by lying or deceit? How can even "little" lies cause disunity? What is the proper way to address lying in the church?

From the Commentary

It is possible to be angry and not sin, but if we do sin, we must settle the matter quickly and not let the sun go down on our wrath. "Agree with thine adversary quickly" (Matt. 5:25). "Go and tell him his fault between thee and him alone" (Matt. 18:15).

—Be Rich, page 124

9. How can people be angry without sinning (4:26–27)? When does anger become sin? What happens when anger is allowed to simmer over time? How does dealing with anger issues right away help to defuse them?

From the Commentary

> The word *corrupt*, used in Matthew 7:17–18, refers to
> rotten fruit. It means "that which is worthless, bad, or
> rotten." Our words do not have to be "dirty" to be worth-
> less. Sometimes we go along with the crowd and try to
> impress people with the fact that we are not as puritani-
> cal as they think.
>
> —*Be Rich*, page 127

10. What is the "unwholesome talke" Paul is referring to in 4:29? Describe
some experiences you've had with this sort of talk. How does this cause disunity? What are the best ways to deal with corrupt or inappropriate talk?

Looking Inward

Take a moment to reflect on all that you've explored thus far in this study
of Ephesians 4. Review your notes and answers and think about how each
of these things matters in your life today.

Tips for Small Groups: To get the most out of this section, form pairs or trios and have group members take turns answering these questions. Be honest and as open as you can in this discussion, but most of all, be encouraging and supportive of others. Be sensitive to those who are going through particularly difficult times and don't press people to speak if they're uncomfortable doing so.

11. What experience do you have with false doctrine? How do you respond when you encounter unfamiliar doctrine? What are some ways you can avoid being influenced by unsound doctrine?

12. Have you taken the time to explore your spiritual gifts? If so, what are they? How do you use them to build unity in your church? Are there ways in which you misuse them? If so, what prompts that and how can you change your behavior so you're a unity-builder? (If you have never explored your spiritual gifts, take some time to do so either on your own or with your group.)

13. As you review Ephesians 4:25–32, which of these five sins do you struggle with most?

a tendency to dominate others

impatience

deceit

unresolved anger

inappropriate talk

What should replace those sins? How will you do that?

Going Forward

14. Think of one or two things that you have learned that you'd like to work on in the coming week. Remember that this is all about quality, not quantity. It's better to work on one specific area of life and do it well than to work on many and do poorly (or to be so overwhelmed that you simply don't try).

Do you need to learn more about your spiritual gifts? Do you need to deal with some of the sins that cause disunity? Be specific. Go back through Ephesians 4 and put a star next to the phrase or verse that speaks to the area you most need to work on. Consider memorizing this verse.

Real-Life Application Ideas: Participate in a spiritual-gifts inventory (ask your pastor for a resource to help with this). Then meet with your small group to discuss your different gifts and how you can use them to build unity.

Seeking Help

15. Write a prayer below (or simply pray one in silence), inviting God to work on your mind and heart in those areas you've previously noted. Be honest about your desires and fears.

Notes for Small Groups:

- *Look for ways to put into practice the things you wrote in the Going Forward section. Talk with other group members about your ideas and commit to being accountable to one another.*

- *During the coming week, ask the Holy Spirit to continue to reveal truth to you from what you've read and studied.*

- *Before you start the next lesson, read Ephesians 5. For more in-depth lesson preparation, read chapters 10 and 11, "Imitating Our Father" and "Heaven in Your Home," in* Be Rich.

Imitation
(EPHESIANS 5)

Before you begin …
- *Pray for the Holy Spirit to reveal truth and wisdom as you go through this lesson.*
- *Read Ephesians 5. This lesson references chapters 10 and 11 in* Be Rich. *It will be helpful for you to have your Bible and a copy of the commentary available as you work through this lesson.*

Getting Started

From the Commentary

If we are the children of God, then we ought to imitate our Father. This is the basis for the three admonitions in this section. God is love (1 John 4:8); therefore, "walk in love" (Eph. 5:1–2). God is light (1 John 1:5); therefore, "walk as children of light" (Eph. 5:3–14). God is truth (1 John 5:6); therefore, walk in wisdom (Eph. 5:15–17).

—*Be Rich*, page 133

1. Why do you think Paul chooses these three admonitions? How do they support his previous teaching on unity?

More to Consider: What are other attributes of God that we, as His children, ought to emulate? List four or five here. How do we emulate these attributes? Is emulating God's attributes enough? How do we move from "emulation" or practicing certain attributes to actually living them out naturally?

2. Choose one verse or phrase from Ephesians 5 that stands out to you. This could be something you're intrigued by, something that makes you uncomfortable, something that puzzles you, something that resonates with you, or just something you want to examine further. Write that here. What strikes you about this verse?

Going Deeper

From the Commentary

> Paul began with "walk in love" because love is the fundamental factor in the Christian life. If we walk in love, we will not disobey God or injure men because "he that loveth another hath fulfilled the law" (Rom. 13:8). The Holy Spirit puts this love in our hearts (Rom. 5:5).
>
> —*Be Rich*, page 135

3. After Paul admonishes his readers to walk in love, he lists a number of behaviors to avoid. List these behaviors (5:3–7). How are these behaviors evidence of not walking in love?

From the Commentary

> In Paul's day, there were false Christians who argued that believers could live in sin and get away with it. These deceivers had many arguments to convince ignorant Christians that they could sin repeatedly and still enter God's kingdom. "You were saved by grace!" they argued. "Therefore

go ahead and sin that God's grace might abound!" Paul answered that foolish argument in Romans 6.

—Be Rich, page 137

4. In Romans 6, Paul argues that for a Christian to desire to sin is crazy—sin is a terrible slavery, and one of the reasons a sane person turns to Christ is to be freed from that slavery. Consider a couple of the sins Paul mentions in Ephesians 5:3–7, such as sexual immorality and greed. How are those sins a form of slavery?

Why would a sane person be eager for Christ to free him from greed, rather than saying to himself, "I'm forgiven by grace, so now I can think and act as greedily as I want without worrying about hell!"?

From the History Books

In 1937, Dietrich Bonhoeffer wrote *The Cost of Discipleship*. In one famous passage he writes, "Cheap grace is preaching forgiveness without requiring repentance, baptism without church discipline, Communion without confession.... Cheap grace is grace without discipleship, grace without the cross, grace without Jesus Christ, living and incarnate." This book was written as Hitler was coming to power, and Bonhoeffer himself became a voice of opposition to Hitler's leadership. Just one month before Germany surrendered, he was hanged along with six other resisters.

5. How was Bonhoeffer's life an example of what he wrote about the cost of discipleship? In what ways does Paul's letter to the Ephesians support Bonhoeffer's teaching about grace?

From the Commentary

> To "walk as children of light" means to live before the eyes of God, not hiding anything. It is relatively easy to hide things from other people because they cannot see our hearts and minds, but "all things are naked and opened unto the eyes of him with whom we have to do" (Heb. 4:13).
>
> —*Be Rich*, page 139

6. Why do people choose to hide things from each other? If we can't hide things from God, why do we try? What does this walking as "children of light" (5:8–13) look like in everyday terms?

From the Commentary

> Only a fool drifts with the wind and tide. A wise man marks out his course, sets his sails, and guides the rudder until he reaches his destination. When a man wants to build a house, he first draws his plans so he knows what he is doing. Yet, how many Christians plan their days so that they use their opportunities wisely?
>
> —*Be Rich*, pages 141–42

7. What are some examples of drifting "with the wind and tide"? How does Paul's admonition in 5:15–16 speak to this tendency? What sort of circumstances do you think Paul was addressing with his admonition to walk as wise? What are some practical ways to do this?

From the Commentary

> Joy is one of the fruits of the Spirit (Gal. 5:22). Christian joy is not a shallow emotion that, like a thermometer, rises and falls with the changing atmosphere of the home. Rather, Christian joy is a deep experience of adequacy and confidence

in spite of the circumstances around us. The Christian can be joyful even in the midst of pain and suffering.

—*Be Rich*, page 149

8. In Ephesians 5:20, Paul says we should be thankful for all things. Do you think he means we should thank God even for a child's death in a car accident? Explain your answer.

Paul spent a lot of time in prison, yet still found joy in his relationship with Christ. He wasn't glad he was in prison, but he found things to be thankful for in his painful and dangerous situation (Phil. 1:12–26). What are modern-day examples of this sort of joy in difficult times? How do these examples support Wiersbe's definition of Christian joy?

More to Consider: Read Ephesians 5:22–27. What does this Scripture passage say about marriage? What is the most important takeaway from these verses? Some people see this passage as controversial because of the word submit. *However, Paul is not diminishing the role of the wife in marriage. In what ways does this passage paint a picture of our desired relationship with Christ?*

From the Commentary

The word *gratitude* comes from the same root word as *grace*. If we have experienced the grace of God, then we ought to be grateful for what God brings to us. *Thank* and *think* also come from the same root word. If we would think more, we would thank more.

—*Be Rich*, page 152

9. What circumstances make thankfulness difficult? How can recognizing the role of grace help you to be thankful?

From the Commentary

To experience the fullness of the Spirit, a person must first possess the Spirit—be a Christian. Then there must be a sincere desire to glorify Christ, since this is why the Holy Spirit was given (John 16:14). We do not use the Holy Spirit; He uses us. There must be a deep thirst for God's fullness, a confession that we cannot do His will apart from His power.

—*Be Rich*, page 157

10. What is your initial reaction to the statement "We do not use the Holy Spirit; He uses us"? How does the Holy Spirit use us? How does He help us as we attempt to imitate Christ?

Looking Inward

Take a moment to reflect on all that you've explored thus far in this study of Ephesians 5. Review your notes and answers and think about how each of these things matters in your life today.

Tips for Small Groups: To get the most out of this section, form pairs or trios and have group members take turns answering these questions. Be honest and as open as you can in this discussion, but most of all, be encouraging and supportive of others. Be sensitive to those who are going through particularly difficult times and don't press people to speak if they're uncomfortable doing so.

11. Go through Ephesians 5 and circle all of Paul's warnings about inappropriate behavior. Silently reflect on how well you're doing at avoiding these behaviors. What does it mean to you to walk in love? How does walking in love help you avoid making poor choices?

12. Are you wishing you could hide things from God? If so, what is prompting that desire? What would it take to trust God with the darker "secrets" of your life? How will you go about doing that?

13. What are some of the challenges you face today that make it difficult for you to be thankful? How might you yet discover true joy in those circumstances?

Going Forward

14. Think of one or two things that you have learned that you'd like to work on in the coming week. Remember that this is all about quality, not quantity. It's better to work on one specific area of life and do it well than to work on many and do poorly (or to be so overwhelmed that you simply don't try). Also, remember that the Holy Spirit is available to help you when you make time for Him and depend on Him.

Do you need to work on walking in love when it comes to your relationship with your spouse? Do you need to cultivate gratitude or find better ways to seek wisdom? Be specific. Go back through Ephesians 5 and put a star next to the phrase or verse that speaks to the area you most need to work on. Consider memorizing this verse.

Real-Life Application Ideas: If you're married, make plans to attend a marriage seminar as soon as possible. (You'll likely spend more than a little time examining this passage in Ephesians.) Or, if you're not married, consider starting a small-group study of Ephesians 5 to explore the implications of Paul's teaching for single people. Invite your pastor to provide supplemental resources on this important Scripture passage.

Seeking Help

15. Write a prayer below (or simply pray one in silence), inviting God to work on your mind and heart in those areas you've previously noted. Be honest about your desires and fears.

Notes for Small Groups:

- *Look for ways to put into practice the things you wrote in the Going Forward section. Talk with other group members about your ideas and commit to being accountable to one another.*

- *During the coming week, ask the Holy Spirit to continue to reveal truth to you from what you've read and studied.*

- *Before you start the next lesson, read Ephesians 6. For more in-depth lesson preparation, read chapters 12 and 13, "Living the Lordship of Christ" and "You're in the Army Now!" in Be Rich.*

Living It
(EPHESIANS 6)

Before you begin ...
- *Pray for the Holy Spirit to reveal truth and wisdom as you go through this lesson.*
- *Read Ephesians 6. This lesson references chapters 12 and 13 in* Be Rich. *It will be helpful for you to have your Bible and a copy of the commentary available as you work through this lesson.*

Getting Started

From the Commentary

It seems no matter where we look in modern society, we see antagonism, division, and rebellion. Husbands and wives are divorcing each other; children are rebelling against their parents; and employers and employees are seeking for new ways to avoid strikes and keep the machinery of industry running productively. We have tried education, legislation, and every other approach, but nothing seems to work. Paul's solution to the antagonisms in the home and in society was *regeneration*—a new heart from God and a new submission to Christ and to one another.

—*Be Rich*, page 161

1. What are some examples of the antagonism, division, and rebellion facing our world today? According to Paul, how do a "new heart" and a "new submission" offer a solution to these problems?

More to Consider: In Ephesians 6, Paul offers suggestions on how Christians can develop spiritual harmony. What is spiritual harmony, and why is it important in the lives of believers?

2. Choose one verse or phrase from Ephesians 6 that stands out to you. This could be something you're intrigued by, something that makes you uncomfortable, something that puzzles you, something that resonates with you, or just something you want to examine further. Write that here. What strikes you about this verse?

Going Deeper

From the Commentary

> There is an order in nature, ordained of God, that argues
> for the rightness of an action. Since the parents brought
> the child into the world, and since they have more knowl-
> edge and wisdom than the child, it is right that the child
> obey his parents. Even young animals are taught to obey.
> The "modern version" of Ephesians 6:1 would be, "Par-
> ents, obey your children, for this will keep them happy
> and bring peace to the home." But this is contrary to
> God's order in nature.
>
> —*Be Rich*, page 162

3. What are other ways in which our society today is at odds with Paul's
teaching in 6:1–4? How does the state of the family in our culture reflect
the truth behind Paul's words?

From the Commentary

> We must be sure, however, that we discipline our children
> in the right manner. To begin with, we must discipline in
> love and not in anger, lest we injure either the body or the
> spirit of the child, or possibly both. If we are not disci-
> plined, we surely cannot discipline others, and "flying off
> the handle" never made a better child or a better parent.
>
> —*Be Rich*, page 166

4. Paul tells his readers to discipline "in the Lord" (6:4). What do you think
this means in practical terms? What does discipline "outside" of Christ look
like? How does a parent discipline in love? How does this sort of wisdom
apply to authorities in general?

From the History Books

As recent as fifty years ago, parenting in the United States was generally a
much different thing than it is today. Though the point is arguable, most
sociologists would likely agree that we have moved from an age where
respect of parental authority was a "given" to a time when parents and
children often compete for authority. Instead of parent-child relationships,

many modern families feature friend-to-friend relationships, eschewing traditional roles.

5. What do you think prompted the shift for many families from a traditional parenting model to one that often trades parental authority for friendship? What are the dangers of being your child's best friend?

From the Commentary

> Jesus said the way to be a ruler is first to be a servant (Matt. 25:21). The person who is not under authority has no right to exercise authority. This explains why many of the great men of the Bible were first servants before God made them rulers: Joseph, Moses, Joshua, David, and Nehemiah are just a few examples. Even after a man becomes a leader, he must still lead by serving.
>
> —*Be Rich*, page 170

6. What does a servant-leader do that differentiates him or her from other leaders? Respond to this comment: "The person who is not under authority has no right to exercise authority."

From the Commentary

> As Christians, we face three enemies: the world, the flesh, and the Devil (Eph. 2:1–3). "The world" refers to the system around us that is opposed to God, that caters to "the lust of the flesh, and the lust of the eyes, and the pride of life" (1 John 2:15–17). "Society apart from God" is a simple, but accurate, definition of "the world." "The flesh" is the old nature that we inherited from Adam, a nature that is opposed to God and can do nothing spiritual to please God.
>
> —*Be Rich*, page 175

7. How do these three enemies manifest in the world around you? What is a Christian's response to these enemies? How do we go about defeating them?

From the Commentary

> The important point is that our battle is not against human beings. It is against spiritual powers. We are wasting our

time fighting people when we ought to be fighting the Devil, who seeks to control people and make them oppose the work of God.

—*Be Rich*, page 177

8. How is a spiritual battle different from battling people? Why do Christians battle other people instead of fighting spiritual battles? Why do you think Paul makes this distinction in Ephesians?

More to Consider: According to Acts 19:23–41, a riot took place during Paul's ministry in Ephesus that could have destroyed the church. Read this passage. Who or what was the cause of the riot? How does this circumstance line up with what Paul is teaching in Ephesians 6?

From the Commentary

In one sense, the "whole armor of God" is a picture of Jesus Christ. Christ is the Truth (John 14:6), and He is our righteousness (2 Cor. 5:21) and our peace (Eph. 2:14).

His faithfulness makes possible our faith (Gal. 2:20); He is our salvation (Luke 2:30); and He is the Word of God (John 1:1, 14). This means that when we trusted Christ, we received the armor.

—*Be Rich*, page 182

9. Review Ephesians 6:13–20. How does knowing we received the armor when we trusted Christ affect the manner in which we use it? What does each piece of the armor do for us? How does the Spirit help us to use them?

From the Commentary

Prayer is the energy that enables the Christian soldier to wear the armor and wield the sword. We cannot fight the battle in our own power, no matter how strong or talented we may think we are.

—*Be Rich*, page 182

10. What happens when we attempt to fight spiritual battles on our own? How does prayer give believers the energy to wear the armor? What are some practical ways to incorporate prayer into our battles?

Looking Inward

Take a moment to reflect on all that you've explored thus far in this study of Ephesians 6. Review your notes and answers and think about how each of these things matters in your life today.

Tips for Small Groups: To get the most out of this section, form pairs or trios and have group members take turns answering these questions. Be honest and as open as you can in this discussion, but most of all, be encouraging and supportive of others. Be sensitive to those who are going through particularly difficult times and don't press people to speak if they're uncomfortable doing so.

11. How well are you applying Paul's teachings from Ephesians 6 in your own relationships? What are some areas you might need to work on? How can you go about that?

12. What is your personal experience with servant leadership? If you are a leader, how well do you follow Paul's model for leadership? What role does humility play in your personal style of leadership?

13. Which item in the "full armor of God" do you feel most comfortable with? Why? How are you using these weapons in your battle to live out the life God calls you to live? What role does prayer play in your spiritual battles?

Going Forward

14. Think of one or two things that you have learned that you'd like to work on in the coming week. Remember that this is all about quality, not quantity. It's better to work on one specific area of life and do it well than to work on many and do poorly (or to be so overwhelmed that you simply

don't try). Remember that the Holy Spirit is available to help you, and that you won't get anywhere without Him.

Do you need to focus on being a better parent? Child? Follower? Leader? Do you need to incorporate more prayer into your life so you can be better prepared for spiritual battles? Be specific. Go back through Ephesians 6 and put a star next to the phrase or verse that speaks to the area you most need to work on. Consider memorizing this verse.

Real-Life Application Ideas: Invite a few close friends to join you in studying Ephesians 6:13–20 and exploring how to use these weapons in a practical sense. Share with each other the sort of battles you're facing, and work together to find a spiritual solution to earthly challenges.

Seeking Help

15. Write a prayer below (or simply pray one in silence), inviting God to work on your mind and heart in those areas you've previously noted. Be honest about your desires and fears.

Notes for Small Groups:

- *Look for ways to put into practice the things you wrote in the Going Forward section. Talk with other group members about your ideas and commit to being accountable to one another.*

- *During the coming week, ask the Holy Spirit to continue to reveal truth to you from what you've read and studied.*

Summary and Review

Notes for Small Groups: This session is a summary and review of this book. Because of that, it is shorter than the previous lessons. If you are using this in a small-group setting, consider combining this lesson with a time of fellowship or a shared meal.

Before you begin...
- *Pray for the Holy Spirit to reveal truth and wisdom as you go through this lesson.*
- *Briefly review the notes you made in the previous sessions. You will refer back to previous sections throughout this bonus lesson.*

Looking Back

1. Over the past eight lessons, you've examined Paul's letter to the Ephesians. What expectations did you bring to this study? In what ways were those expectations met?

2. What is the most significant personal discovery you've made from this study? How does this discovery affect the way you view Paul's letter to the Ephesians? How are you like or unlike the recipients of this letter?

3. What was most inspiring to you about Paul's explanation of the riches of Christ? In what ways are you enjoying and employing those riches in your everyday life?

Progress Report

4. Take a few moments to review the Going Forward sections of the previous lessons. How would you rate your progress in each of the areas you chose to work on? What adjustments, if any, do you need to make to continue on the path toward spiritual maturity?

5. In what ways have you grown closer to Christ during this study? Take a moment to celebrate those things. Then think of areas where you feel you still need to grow and note those here. Make plans to revisit this study in a few weeks to review your growing faith.

Things to Pray About

6. Ephesians is a book packed with practical help for Christians who seek to live richly. As you reflect on the words Paul wrote, ask God to reveal to you those truths that you most need to hear. Revisit the book often and seek the Holy Spirit's guidance to gain a better understanding of what it means to be rich before God.

7. The messages in Ephesians cover a wide variety of topics, including peace, the mystery of faith, unity, imitating Christ, and learning how to live a life of faith in practical ways. Spend time praying about each of these topics.

8. Whether you've been studying this in a small group or on your own, there are many other Christians working through the very same issues you've discovered while examining Paul's letter to the Ephesians. Take time to pray for them, that God would reveal truth, that the Holy Spirit would guide you, and that each person might grow in spiritual maturity according to God's will.

A Blessing of Encouragement

Studying the Bible is one of the best ways to learn how to be more like Christ. Thanks for taking this step. In closing, let this blessing precede you and follow you into the next week while you continue to marinate in God's Word:

May God light your path to greater understanding as you review the truths found in the book of Ephesians and consider how they can help you grow closer to Christ.

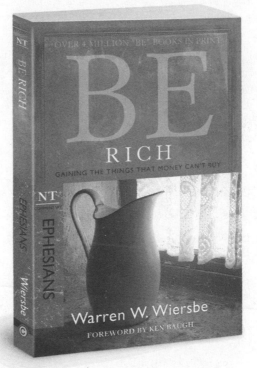

The "BE" series . . .

For years pastors and lay leaders have embraced Warren W. Wiersbe's very accessible commentary of the Bible through the individual "BE" series. Through the work of David C. Cook Global Mission, the "BE" series is part of a library of books made available to indigenous Christian workers. These are men and women who are called by God to grow the kingdom through their work with the local church worldwide. Here are a few of their remarks as to how Dr. Wiersbe's writings have benefited their ministry.

"Most Christian books I see are priced too high for me . . .
I received a collection that included 12 Wiersbe
commentaries a few months ago and I have
read every one of them.
I use them for my personal devotions every day and they
are incredibly helpful for preparing sermons.
The contribution David C. Cook is making to the
church in India is amazing."

—Pastor E. M. Abraham, Hyderabad, India

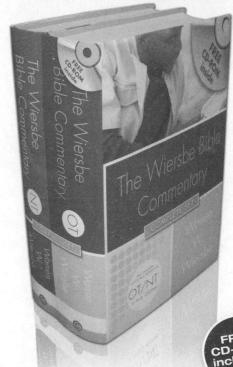